MW00784033

DEAD HORSE

DEAD HORSE

NIINA POLLARI

BIRDS, LLC | AUSTIN, MINNEAPOLIS, NEW YORK, RALEIGH

Birds, LLC
Austin, Minneapolis, New York, Raleigh
www.birdsllc.com

Copyright © 2015 by Niina Pollari
All rights reserved

Cover designed by Josh Elliott
Interior designed by Michael Newton

Library of Congress Cataloging-in-Publication Data:
Pollari, Niina
Dead Horse/Niina Pollari
Library of Congress Control Number: 2014940781

First Edition, 2015
ISBN-13: 9780991429813
Printed in the United States of America

CONTENTS

MONEY

I AM SKINLESS IN A LIMO

A little bit of context:
I am skinless in a limo
But I have like a dress on
It's a green dress like a bird from a very green place

Because I have no skin
I am afraid of touching the sour door handle
I'm very vulnerable
I can't really leave

But my friend
When I think about you
I am having a hard time understanding

You see
We lost touch
When we were children in a faraway country:

You and me
Orange-tan and happy
I was eating tiny fried fish at the square
Grinding up their mini-mini skeletons
Chewing their soft spines
With my teeth
All day

It was such a sunny day
The sun was petting us
I didn't have to lick you
I didn't have to do anything I didn't want

But that was back when I had skin

Now I'm sad and nasty
Grafting on to the seat
Wetly in a long car
As outside it rains
And is also
A twister

If I went into the rainstorm now
All of me would wash off except my dress
Which would be ruined
The green fluff turning to soggy brown
Covered with the red of my body

It's so good knowing
Your inevitability

The skin is the largest organ in the body
It breathes and eats on its own
And it's very talkative
And I miss it
In the quiet car

But there is no changing the present
And there is no fucking with what happened
So here is a statement of the facts:

My friend is somewhere else
And I am skinless in a limo
And we are headed down

BONES

NATURE POEM

I started a poem
"I am a windstorm"
It was hard

Nature bores me
The way a thing I don't understand bores me
Like when I looked at an article about plagiarism
Sometimes I just can't think about something
I can only describe it with words

A wind that is fussing the windowsill
Is "Words"

The man on the other couch
It's obvious that I don't wish him harm
But I can't talk very well
Because very squalidly built
Is the slum of my words

I eat it all
And invert
And sink back into the couch like a monster
I will become longer
Than my terror eventually

TO THE BONE

Please make me a Bailey's coffee
I really need it
I feel really bad

Please don't stare, I don't feel good
I lifted that line out of a teenager's blog

Anyway call me when you want to scrutinize someone
Because I am it

The girl who heard there'd be drugs and showed up earnestly
Not even "the girl" but "a girl"

And now I'm nothing
But a massive garbage mountain
Wiggling abundantly

And all I want to know is
Do you love me
Now that I can dance

EVEN IN A LANA

I look at pictures of myself sometimes
And I can see my skeleton
Skull all hard
Around the eyes
Where they sink in a little
These pictures are rare but becoming less so

It's blue around the eye sockets
Like a mortal gleam

I can be plain-spoken when I have to be
When I see the network of capillaries mewling close
    to the surface

Over time there will be less and less youthful pictures of me
    until I perish

Lana Del Rey says: "I love the look of girls with red lips
    and shiny skin"
She says this after she poses for British GQ naked
Her butt smashed up against a floor surface
Hugging her knees to her chest
Covering her vagina and stomach

I love this woman I think
But she must be lying right now
This cannot be what she is thinking
Sitting there looking just like how my brain thinks
Being my brain twin on the magazine
Covering the exact right two things

Because even though as a person I'm not
As a woman I'm just so

I'm confused because if I was in that white room
And I put on red lips and shiny skin I would feel wrong
Foody and gleaming
Roasting
Creamy
Uncomfortably warm
I would want to minimize the surface
Like she's doing

Looking fucked up in a photo is hard

Under the skin
The soft skin I allegedly own
That is disappearing from me every day
That is a temporary boon for me and my loves to touch

Is a skeleton

Under the vagina and guts
Even in a Lana
A skeleton hides

Ready to grin in your face
Ready to fuck your shit up like a nightmare
Ready to be a pile of dead bones in the moonlight

I WANT

I want everyone to stay away from me
If they can't touch me in a way I like
In a way that feels like a teddybear being thrown at my face
Yes, like with fat and fur
In your fingers

It clambers down my face
Like a child hand

Then I make you a cake out of stuff that falls off my body
You can believe it's presentable and fine
And it's all eaten

It was a good party
We say grimly and wet ourselves on the chair

I am a caricature and you are an armature
And one of us can get bent

DEAD HORSE

In the thunder, in the thunder covering the water
And the lightning fingering down from the sky
Am I

A shade
Your face is growing familiar
I have seen it before somewhere

The sky glares green
On the wet road the swish of tire pulls to a stop

Something comes here to die

It's always like this
Lights first
Then noise

Facing the pathless darkness
Darkening more
Don't talk

It feels like noise
From headphones, in the air
In my hand, static

We stand still as coins
Silent

The apocalypse I feel
Is turning itself up like snow
On a dead channel

A breeze inflates itself from the water
Rotten in the nose
But dear in the skeleton

Dear
As a bone saw

As bits of bone that angle up from the ground
Where they were buried
Are bits of mine and bits of yours

A faraway plane flies over their everlasting shards like a bird
Like the atmosphere, pieced with three-dimensional gulls

Having become familiar

They have seen me before somewhere as they have seen you
As I have seen you

The pieces of birds will stand in for something
And if now you have to leave, you know
I will lay down in the rotten road
And wait for you until you come

My friend
I am lonely

Without you
The killing night comes down
Like a horse from heaven

I am sitting on it like a divan

The night is a ghost cracking
Its long unhinged jaw in my ear

Your voice
In the rotten air

If you say you love me
I will open my mouth and you can live in it

If you need it abandoned leave it with me
I am so happy
To take it

If I am your friend then I am proud
If I am proud then I love it
If I love it
Then I am dying all the time

If all the time
I had died all the time
I would have had you come back

And in the bony night I would hold the elbow of my friend
And grateful would I learn to speak

So I want what happens

To darken my heart for good

In the bay

By our dead horse

Without you

I go a little weird

Your face
Your familiar face

I touch the bones of your face
I touch the lingering feeling of the bones of your face
Like a pieta

Long moments after you have gone
I am still doing it

The air stretched tight like a drum

Face of the water, the long face of water

Big air
With seagulls rising into it
Bone shards rising into it
Filaments thin as thread from my fingers rising into it

A RED THING

The butts of my palms are almost the exact shape
Of my eye sockets

And when I press them down
Out come the colors from behind my lids
It's laughably simple
To control what your eyes see this way

Anyone can do it
You don't have to be a sorcerer

You can be anyone – just say uh-oh!
My eyes are seeing things
Some gray things
A big pink thing
Followed by a red thing!

Because everything always ends with a red thing

BLOOD

PERSONAL PAIN

Today I had an IUD placed
It was one stinging pain
Followed by one long pain
Followed by nothing

I visualized a wall anchor
I think this made it worse

The pain was not transcendent
As much as I would have liked for it to be
Wanting transcendence through pain is a deep wish I always have
I know I am not alone there

The pain was oddly personal, internal
Not to be described as "touch"

More like a recoil from a memory
Of unpleasant touch but not something that shifts you
Or even wavers you at all

I've looked for big shifting pain
Shiny incomparable pain since I was a kid
This sounds braggy but I only mean
I sat in front of a mirror piercing my ears with an ice cube
    and safety pin

Four or five times until the infections came
And the metal allergy and later a large tattoo that I sat for
In anticipation

Just like this
My device's insertion
At the second flash of sear, the nurse heard
My inhale and looked at me and said "Are you OK"
"I'm fine," I said "Thanks for asking"

PRAYER, ON FIRE

Pick it to a scab
Small wounded moment

Thin and bright as a Coors
Light poured into a glass, throwing
Fog

Here we suddenly have a wild
Calm: brown and orange, the sap
In the receptacle, and thirst, now
Is an animal somehow

Going under, handsome
As a classical patient, in spite
Of all of technology's fail

Repeat after me, blog it if you want

The thermals of the earth are neverending, neverending
Something about the Gulfstream
The oppression you feel
Et cetera

THE BLOOD

When I go to sleep in a house
I know I'm gonna be a goblin

As in the night, in all homes
I always wake myself up starting to bleed

On the good thread-count sheet
The symbol of it in dreams
So boring to talk about dreams
But blood, that tiresome perennial
Succubus/goblin

In the dream
I leave blood on each chair that I sit in
A web trails from me when I get up, forever
It's tied to me like an immaculate dove
Tied to the ear of Mary the Jesus Mom

The walk I'm walking in my dream
Makes a lengthening gunk from me to my chair

I'm a nastyish goblin
But it feels so significant
That I guess you could say it's a wet dream

REPOSSESSING THE ZOMBIE

The static washing over
A continuous whinny
I can't, obligation

I was supposed to be
The courthouse, I was supposed

To be the somnambulist

You should
Never startle walking sleepers
On the TV they are saying *the heart*

is actually more like a pine cone
covered in individual scales, each one
harboring a small brown seed
the way one conceals a fugitive

NO EMERGENCY

A reflection of the letters
Of my computer's backlit keyboard
Glitters in the airplane's double-pane window

The reflection splays across the sky like some stars
My fingers move across them like a solar darkness

I am famished
I used up all of my body getting to the airport
I have this entire row of seats to myself but I'm claiming one
And in it, my body sits tight and small
Like one good line

A plane is amazing
With all its adjustable knobs, to give us the feeling of control
And all the really dangerous parts
Left unmoved

For example I could turn a reading light on
Or put my magazine away into the secure hug of the pocket in front of me
Or move my seat back and fold my body on it to sleep
But right outside one pressure-shut lever
That wild wind

Earlier I left behind a warm apartment
And a man whom I love and for whom I feel gratitude

For whom
On mornings in bed I feel
A breaking tenderness

He was cooking dinner for himself when I left
And making a little extra, he's practical that way
"Do you have time to stay and eat," he asked
And when I said no he said
"Do you have the money for a cab, you should never be afraid
    to ask me"

And I thought
I have this

As I locked the door behind me
My throat feeling like the little waist
Between the segments of a wasp's body

At home in bed
I have messy dreams that wake me
And I look at my body shining in the floodlight from the car lot next door

Sometimes the lonely part of my heart pings
And I get super afraid
And turn

I thread my arm around the body
With its back to me, and I put my hand on the heart

This is not supposed to sound heavy-handed
But I get that it does
But I just need proof, you know
Something that lets me press my chest on it and feel okay

The light weirds the room when it looks in like that
My body is the thing that belongs to me the least

Inside the plane, the lights go dim

I can't stop thinking of how I'm hurtling through the sky

My computer is running on reserve power
I am too

There's no place to plug into
There's nothing in the night
But air
Cold high air
Negative air in unfathomable temperatures

I am cold and feel lonely
And like I want something

At my seat I have a cup of water and a stack of napkins

The light from my window is safe and tiny
And brightens pretty much nothing outside

My body is a closet
My body is smaller than a closet
My body is folded into an airplane's overhead bin
My body is so close to dying

Everyone sleeps around me

I never sleep on planes because I don't feel right
But it's sort of comfortable now and I can get close
I let my hands rest

And as they do
The keyboard light goes out
The reflection in the window stops moving

And this stops the battery
From draining entirely

YOU MUST FLOSS TO READ

I flossed with a cherry dental thread, spit and closed my eyes
The agonizingly long time
That it takes blood to make it down the drain

I can't look
It can't be this easy
The human version

Of fake champagne, atomized
Somebody likes it
A toxifying mist

Like the pheromone slam
Of drugstore perfume
Sexifying
Spritzed to attract but then near
The epicenter that dry-heaving chemical thing

Come closer and closer so that everybody gets some
It's so tiring and sentimental

Nearness and farness are the same when your reaction doesn't change
Just the order of things matters

Like now
My gums, blood containers, lie stripped in my mouth
The water has washed their giving away
And I will put this book in front of me

Now I will read the last word first
And this will change what the book is about

FUTURE KITCHEN MAXIM

A human like a human from a stove
Is like the hot hand down my body now
It's like a poem about inevitability

We encountered in the kitchen

And a grain burns
A grain burns on the range

Not a grain, but actually a strange unraveling seed

Open the bucket
And stir around the slime

Eggshells can't be trampled if I don't save them first
But I haven't saved them first

I LOVE MY GUT

My gut sits low on my body
It's substantial and forgiving
I love my gut
It's going to help me so much through these hard times
It softly hums to me before I fall asleep
In the darkness I like to listen to it sing
It goes
"Hum hum"

I love it because it cares
It doesn't see, but yet it sees
It helped me feel a lot less lonely in college
It really helped me feel a lot less lonely in grad school
It helped me feel pretty OK when I was emotional about a man
The notion of the gut as a seat of emotions is ancient
It explains phrases like "gut reaction"

I would never twist it
I would never suck it away or shrink it
I don't have that murdering instinct in me like some do
I would just feel too too bad

Oh, baby gut
We are together forever
I really respect you
During these hard times

I will make you a crown, lie down on the floor then put it on you
And stay real still except for breathing and watch you move up and down

TIGER HANDS

Don't trust what a tiger
Told you
Never

Tiger hands
Ruin things
Tiger hands are a personal gun

For example I want to be over there
Want to listen to a nice song with you
Be good
:)
But for my tiger hands

Tiger hands grab hold hard for eating
Tiger face is not even needed

I don't have a tiger face as you can see
But that's why I usually kill way more than I need
Before my brain and face
Actually realize what I did

MY PREGNANCY

I fold my hands across my belly
It is deceptive I know
It causes people to think things, those times when I
Have a glass of wine in my hand

I am not expecting a baby but I like to pretend and people care much more

I hold the wine glass up high like a ceremony while
My other hand rests carefully
And iconically across my upper abs

I tuck my lower spine in
Cultivate a loving lordosis

It's funny how much your body makes you think of yourself
For example whenever I do this
I start to feel staggering
Protective feelings over my bladder
I guess you could say I am a very nurturing human being

VAMPIRE

I am a vampire in a grayly coughing dawn
I prepare a ritual of the hallucinogenic sleep
I lay down and spread
My gnatted arms by my sides
I cannot
But let
An Autobahn of blood be mealy in me

You know what I mean
We king our impulses, love
Eat and prey
Every day

It's a fakey arcade
And I am its operator laughing copper with blood in my teeth
I spin a bright novelty ball on my finger
While I watch you watch me

I can't make myself be alive
I do not feel sorry
I only talk about me
The laptop shudders violently when I type my About Me

You ask if I will stay here in the ruin
With you, and of course I will

When I say those words exactly
I let them rope out of my mouth
And twine around my fingers

What I do is a conjunction

I smooth the gothic filament of my agreeing
And I close my eyes

And how an hourglass is wide on both ends
But wide enough in the center for one grain only
That image is my voice
Working in my throat

I use it to gorge you
With my gentle introduction
"I can smell you
It's nice and I like it
Did you know that I am real"

IT'S OK TO HAVE NO HEART

Deep under the muscle
Is one cold place
A diuretic place
Where the water rushes opposite gravity

Like, you know what it is about something leaving you
Really leaving you

The moment when you've breathed in all the air you can breathe
And you then take in one more sip, and something breaks a little
In your sternum
There you are
Breathing a little less easy
Inhaling a little more shaky

Uneasily watching Illuminati videos on YouTube
Getting real weird and down

For you my audience
If you are still with me, I want
To tell you what it will be like when it leaves
There's a sense of discovery
But it's not sentimental
You'll find
Something hidden
But most of you will die

DO YOU FEEL TENDERNESS

When I went to the doctor
I forgot to take off my bra
She said "Oh! I'm sorry, I need to check
Your breast tissue"
Yes, I said, I'm so sorry

I had a hard time unclasping the hooks and eyes
I didn't look at the doctor, who was a new lady doctor
I met ten minutes before, at the start of my appointment
Finally I took off my bra
So many wolves fell out

In the roaring of the wolves the doctor said "Do you feel tenderness"
She was touching me

No, I said, not mostly
She said "You have very fibrous breast tissue I would not be surprised
If you felt tenderness during your period"

And the wolves ran around the table like a dog pack
Screaming and howling
In that little room

I said I don't have a period, then we barely locked eyes, the end

TEARS FOR FEARS

He says with his hand

On the back of my neck

In some new place where

I was dropped off, O

Unable now to go

To the girl I was before

Powerless before

The Saigon of my corpuscles

Wet before any of the rain even came

He was very handsome

With a fist for kissing

And now I kiss America

With my green face and cry

The minute I am done

SWAN'S BLOOD

I am next to you
I put my thigh meat next to yours
I have a swan's blood inside my mouth, so I just smile
The warmth from your thigh will seep into mine
The sturdiness I have
My predator's leg

I will sit quietly

Like an animal
Enjoying the warm sunlight with blood in my mouth

I'm not a monster
If I seem like one
It's because nobody ever said no

The swan's blood is being watered down with my saliva
Til it's thin and pink

My fingernails itch to prick through to your legs

But I'm not going to
I'm not going
To be a beast

I close my teeth
And my lips over my teeth
And the blood will stay inside and you are spared

My love and the world keeps on ringing with sunshine

MONEY

MANIFESTO

See, once I was very young and had very long hair
And so I was big enough to hold everything
Now I am much older
And smaller
And shrinking all the time

I stand in a room
Let the music
Yes let

The music
Rinse over me

Sometimes your world, it gets smaller
And less populated so you make more with less
And yes more art even
With less people

So now look, witness
What's the awful thing happening

It closed the door
It cost my friends their lives with me

In the place of friends
Is a familiar tree of feelings
Grown and green and a big canopy
Misanthropically dense and brushed

Under it I hold a cartoonish mallet
I was good once
But never again

So listen to me
As I rap this

Listen
As I eat my words

I either have to eat them or I will turn blue
I either have to turn away you or your art

BEAUTIFUL LETTERS

A man came up to me on Myrtle
Said "Excuse me sister
I hate to even ask you this but it's for a baby"
I gave him what he needed though I don't know how it goes
He said he would go with me to the shop
Watch me charge the formula
"You know what infant formula is right"
I know what infant formula is
This isn't about me or about beautiful letters
Or even the emptiness of refusal
Or the hollow gesture of a dollar
This isn't about me
I'm repeating myself
Me and my layer of fat

I OWE MONEY

I owe money, a large amount
Tied to my name, and following me around
The hundreds of dollars I relinquish every month
I don't even miss it

Paying money is a part of me
Like my human face
The amoebic debt that sparkles around me
Like a beautiful shirt

Recently I counseled a collaborator
From a Socialist Democracy
She was lamenting a homeowner's loan
How it felt like a lot
And a burden

I said: "Debt is always and always will be"
And she began to feel happier, maybe
At the prospect of accepting this beautiful permanence
And more okay about owning her debt

It was a longer and more nuanced conversation
But that was the point of it I think

In Old High German the word owe is tied to ownership
Own is to possess
Owe is to own

Like: I own a bookshelf of narrow poetry volumes
Or: I own a refined Arabian show horse
(I don't)

Ownership is gathering things
And gathering things is a kind of self-definition
So just like that, I have gathered debt
And so I own money and let it define me

A part of me is money
And a part of me is the shadow-money of debt

Picture: a skeleton holding money
Or a boatful of money afloat on the mythical river of death
Free of current

Flanked by a silent swan, the color of a pale wrist
That cuts through the river's unrippled surface

Although once it was, yes
Still long ago money ceased to be a symbol for gold
So we can now make from it a symbol for the purposes of this poem

Still, to make a metaphor only of death is unfair
Because this money is also very alive
When I take money out from a lender as debt
It makes additional money

It generously lends to other people
And creates more of itself into circulation
As it takes part in a process known as fractional reserve banking

Money is made and then deposited into banks again
Sometimes it's used for houses and other large things
Maybe even, appropriately
To finance the arrival of a baby

Life, my friends
Is given to others by my borrowing

It's a fucked up system based on an empty signifier
But still I gather debt around my physical body
Like when you're walking up some stairs in an impossible gown

Like Jennifer Lawrence falling down at the Oscars
Everyone agreed that was a fucking disaster
But she came out of it looking like a sweetie because she accepted
The responsibility of her Dior with a graceful smile

So when you are ascending the steps
With your armfuls of debt dress
And you gather it
(This metaphor is only truly meaningful to women
And those who own feminine clothes)

The debt is not only gorgeous
It is giving meaning to you
Which in turn gives other people what they need

It's awful when you think of debt as a benevolent force
Or an enhancing characteristic or accessory
To talk yourself into having it

Every month I pay my debt
I guess I have a sense of duty about it
I pay it in chunks
Of a few hundred dollars

But every time I do
The money my debt created shrinks from society
Is taken out of circulation, and essentially disappears

Debt creates money
Paying it off destroys money

Repayment destroys both your own money and your debt
And the abundance of everyone else in a debt economy
A debt economy depends on debt to flourish
Even though it's a gloomy abundance
Based in destruction

The goddess Lakshmi is associated with wealth
And she is depicted holding coins and lotuses
She has four arms
And she is constantly distributing her coins with her four hands

Lakshmi is the spouse to Vishnu, the maintainer
And a sort of financier of his maintenance of the universe
I don't pretend to know Hindu mythology very well
But I do know that her generosity
Is fundamental to the world

So, debt and fractional reserve banking
And the etymology of the word "owe" in this light:

It is money, debt
Creation and destruction
And my power as a woman in one tidy metaphor

When I learned that when I pay my debt back
The money I created also reaches to destroy its ninefold
    shadow money
I felt so sad

Sad for my participation in this anti-creation
And for the economic model that created it to begin with
I am creating and destroying, when what I'd like to be doing
    is maintaining

Every two years or so, my loan is sold
And I receive two letters

One from my old provider saying that the loan is paid off
And one from my new provider with instructions on how
   to send them the payment
Every time, I feel a surge
Of joy, and then a sinking

It feels a little thuggish to have my emotions toyed with like this
But I guess I signed up for it when I was eighteen:

That something I owe, and own
Is also owned by someone else

The idea of co-ownership is very domestic
So I guess it's a kind of love in that way
As long as I make my payments
I'm in a kind of love with a corporation

My debt is an emotional experience, too
Since I'm that kind of animal

It has been relatively positive for me
For which I feel lucky
I have always had enough money to make the minimum
So I have never encountered my lover's wrath
It has been peaceful
At least

So I can't imagine how it will feel when this ends
Or what I will do to grieve the relationship I will lose

But I feel that it may be dramatic
In the way that you feel strongly about losing
Suddenly a pattern

Remember the barge in the dark river
I mentioned at the beginning of this poem

Imagine maybe there is another boat
Aflame as it drifts away
And I am the one who set it on fire

My debt
Once a creator
My co-collaborator
Now destroyed by my hand
As I stand at the bank

No longer dual with my majestic dying money
Cold and free and alone

TO THE SPECIALISTS

This is the story of when
I thought about slipping then I did
I have always had a very connected relationship
With my body

So I'm sure when that banana peel
Showed itself to the corner of my eye like a practical joke
My eye told a message to my neurons

That's how it works: be
Prepared to slip
So there was a peel I saw
So then my heel
Slid on the Metrocard
And it was no real surprise

The muscles of my shoulders are tight
Tight and sometimes painful
I went to the doctor and he was like
"How many hours do you spend at the computer"
"13, 14" I said

He said "You have to take the time
To go and walk around and move your body and stuff"
"OK" I said "I'll get a smartphone"

That's what I was doing when I thought
About slipping and I slipped I
Thought about slipping then I
Thought about
Data plans

Then I slipped, it's important to be
Honest with your readers, it's like a doctor and patient
Kind of confidentiality relationship
And where would I be if not for doctors

I am constantly exercising
This special relationship I have
With my body where it and I
Talk all the time, and part of that
Is going
A lot
To the specialists

I LOVE THE PHONE

I live for the phone
I awake every day thinking "I will kill myself if nobody calls
    or texts me today"
My guts do a little nervous dance whenever it's not vibrating
I have such great vibes

You're looking at me like I'm not smart
But you don't even know
I stop existing if nobody reaches out to me

When you, a person, call me, I am more beautiful
And worth more as another person
And more full of living vitamins
And incredibly valuable

It's more meaningful than when we hang out
In real life or in person because there is an actual
Traceable electronic trail

And when the archaeologists find me they can see all the times
    that people called or texted
And they can say to themselves
"She was very beloved"

SMARTPHONE

Some days you can't do anything
Not even your own makeup

Some days you already blew it
One wonkily painted eye
Watching the liner tutorial
Like an unwrapped egg

Leave the house

Then sulk around doing that weird wandering walk
That people do when they're looking at a smartphone
One zombie foot clubbing in front of the next
And your visual anchor gone

Smartphone
Beloved vista
The only real doing is swiping
It's not possible to stay away any longer
The song tightens around you as it tightens around me
All the time

Pure self-definition
Fresco of things I can't forget To-Do

We live in, um, electron air
We live in, um, an election year

NONE OF THIS IS APPETIZING

Westward there is a highway
That some people have to drive on, straight lines
Like a good haircut

Who isn't seeking a beating?
A discount on pharmaceuticals
From a stranger with a weird name, I need
A beating, click yes

To be sent a reminder
I need a reminder, the dead
Letter box is filled with cards that say
Great scenery wish u were nearer
In pathetic script

In a city (beautiful)
The weather approaches (bad)
A stage of almost
Gilded emergency

Staying indoors
Is the only way to stay free
Of mud and pollen, ice tongues
And melt

Out there is sad
And dark, one big
Away message

I used to see feeders
But not anymore

SELF-LOVE IS IMPORTANT

In the night I sit
With a cup of old wine
Tearing me up
It's terrible to admit
I haven't left the house today or gotten dressed
I don't know what yellow the moon is
Or the tail of clouds around it
Or what is a moon
Forgetting is easy: just never go out

Really soon the sun too will become an elaborate metaphor

Yes when we're dead we come apart
A little at a time

Today my exposure
To wilderness is a zooming house fly
And the smell of my own sweat

Hey, creature
I am too poor to kill
The death of a body means nothing
Unless it's your own

And basically the deal is until I get to the end of this poem, or any poem
And/or until I have no more body parts to give
We can both live

Self-love is looking
At yourself like a foreign bug and still loving
I hate my long-dead body, I think every morning and night
Shuddering wine or black coffee down my neck
Pulling it down with gravity
With the grace of gravity
I feel less and fear

Paroxysm, bless
The nerves down
To the feet that fold from my body like serifs

I am going to love something to the ground for once

DEAR SUITOR

When arriving in their SmartCar
To where I was sitting on my divan
Did you think I would be a human being

Did you think it was a girl I would be

A girl to sweetly
Take your dark headphones to crowd you
As you're listening to your dark music
To soothe your dark self

You are like an accordion
Full of borrowed air
Puffed up
Fake big

Where I am a dark stone with a reservoir
Containing blood that no hand will ever reach
And nobody with a daisy in his teeth
Will floss his way into me
Of that he can be sure

WHO IN CLASSICAL LITERATURE
COULD HAVE SAID THIS

The greatest and the most fearful

Like a dumb blade against the carotid
Wielded by a scaredy-cat

Garish movement but not too garish
For fear of further detachment

"The end of philosophy"

We said in a conversation we will always be friends
But what did you think of the video I sent you

Then I shamble my hands across the appalled keys of a synth
Like the video's small animal star

And in a painterly gesture
Your face is blank and you turn it
Towards the broken fence of city sky not comfortably dark
Though it is well after dark
Oh well

PICTURES OF ME

I've been looking so long at these pictures of me that
    I almost believe they are real

What a masterful collection

Dandruff-smelling blanket
Leggings in soft-focus

Me picking the organics then eating them in my dream office
    and that's how

I am like this: one blonde and one brunette steal each others'
    Archies and so begins a beautiful lifelong friendship punctuated
    by occasional, loud fighting and that's me

Usually people think the hair on my sweater is cat hair

When I tear off pieces of my cuticles I eat them because
    I don't want them to end up abandoned

I am nothing like a worthless drunk
Several analysts depend on me in a room
I am a shining example of great possibility
I have a degree and I haven't died of hypothermia
I know how to dress myself
A luminous aura of mystery surrounds me like yoga as I
    address great people
Anyone could see it if they ask, but do not touch these pictures of me

I'm considering installing gallery lighting

Please, nobody touch anything

FOOTBALLS

Footballs are flying through the air
Each football is partnerless and hesitates
Wavering
Til a second one comes from the atmosphere

Footballs are flying through the air

Footballs are hitting children until they cry

For now begin every line with feel

Like feeling was something you actually did very well

Footballs make us feel real

You're like three-week-old laundry
Feel it
And the footballs don't stop and you've got to walk
Past the signs

So significant
Your wrinkles showed themselves just this year

It's November the sky happens to be unreliably tossed
Try to not

Be a wordless failure and you will make it

Through the football rain

Through the mess

But hurtling through any kind of space yes there are always
    footballs to dodge

So dodge them
Obstacle map
You will need some money and tools

The higher the difficulty level

The more vaguely inspiring the ending

ASAFOETIDA

You have one bright blue eye like a hurricane over water
And one brown, like David Bowie

So I don't think you can blame me
For trapping you stone fox
In retrospect it was cold

Inside that fridge, but we hugged a lot

FLORIDA

The imported shoreline is washed away each year
Your feet in the sand
That's trucked and ferried in
The stump of your ankle when you walk

How far to dig in the packed backyard
Before we hit the sand
Can we bury this animal
Deep so other animals won't come

Soon another storm will come
You wrap my arms around
Yourself

Fake romance with you and the storm
Trace the outline of the sea
Your spine growing crooked
Your eyes rolling up

Only 15% of a wave is the visible part
I swim right here but not for long
Thinks everybody about Florida

The iron-scented air
Makes you remember the cigarette you stole during a storm
In more vivid detail
Than the one you smoked in good weather

This is how unjust personal memory is
Wriggling on the end of the hook
You know the hook

You miss so much of your own life
Bank account drawn
Face drawn

More than X years of my life I have had this artistic pressure
To do super well and it all started there
In the lifted offices of Florida
Show your ass
Learn the Arabic of line & meter

Get good evaluations
Get a good book idea
There is an alligator in every ditch in Florida
You can be a good book writer and still get eaten and chewed

Fake romance with you and the alligator
The novelist in you would save the headline

Every pillhead
Is someone's
And could have been yours

I am not a stripper
I am not a pillhead
I am an alligator-headed book writer
Digging a hole in the backyard
For no other animals but the ones in my body

There is a fake romance happening with me and the shovel
I love it and our shared task
And the real results

I am writing
As I dig in the sand
You should see how well I can use tools
Don't you trust me to record this

TRUST MEETING

A smiling prophet slides onto a folding chair
There are currents muddying the water's surface outside
But underground we don't feel it

I touch the metal bar of my own chair, wait for it
To shock me though I know it's illogical
"Logic led me to the grave once" I think completely stupefyingly

In front of me a buck-toothed young man says that I can trust him

This is a workshop for trust
Every weekend I drive past the Tappan Zee
My head kind of thick with confusion
Thinking I could trust someone
If I really tried

My hands on the steering wheel are at ten and two
The bones of my neck ache forward
I drive past the lake and park in the yard

I still think that I could

Trust someone that is

My eyes have that squinting look of trust
And a hopeful tinted disc laid over the cornea

The chair won't get warm but I am going to keep transferring
Pressure makes heat
I want to be warm
The boy in front of me, I take his hand

Inside my mind I say: *Look me in the eyes*
I've known this whole time about the currents
We drove here to forcefully trust each other

And the underground water filters
Beneath our chairs and the floor and never stops
I think about it repeatedly saying:

I Never I Never I Never

I can't look away from the center of his contacts
I am going to never say I can't again

Versions of a few poems from this book appeared in
Finery, The Lumberyard, Tuli&Savu and in a chapbook
called *Fabulous Essential*.

Thank you to Nikolai Basarich, Gina Abelkop, Tytti
Heikkinen, Matt Rasmussen, Sampson Starkweather,
Chris Tonelli, Dan Boehl, Justin Marks, Minna Pollari,
JD Scott, Nicole Steinberg, Zane Van Dusen,
and Judy Berman.

Niina Pollari lives in Brooklyn and has written
two previous chapbooks: *Fabulous Essential* (Birds
of Lace 2009) and *Book Four* (Hyacinth Girl 2012).
She translated Tytti Heikkinen's *The Warmth of the
Taxidermied Animal* (Action Books 2013).